Rodgers and Hammerstein's
THE KING AND I

Souvenir Folio Edition

Featuring scenes from the 1996 Broadway production

Shall We Dance? Lou Diamond Phillips and Donna Murphy

Production photographs by Joan Marcus

Applications for performance of this work, whether legitimate,
stock, amateur or foreign should be addressed to:

THE RODGERS & HAMMERSTEIN THEATRE LIBRARY
229 West 28th Street, 11th floor • New York, NY 10001
Phone: (212) 564-4000
Fax: (212) 268-1245

WILLIAMSON MUSIC®

A RODGERS AND HAMMERSTEIN COMPANY

EXCLUSIVELY DISTRIBUTED BY

HAL•LEONARD®
CORPORATION
7777 W. BLUEMOUND RD. P.O. BOX 13819 MILWAUKEE, WI 53213

The Small House of Uncle Thomas

CONTENTS

Hello, Young Lovers: **Donna Murphy, Taewon Kim, Royal Wives**

I Whistle a Happy Tune: **Donna Murphy, John Curless, Ryan Hopkins**

My Lord and Master: **Joohee Choi**

Randall Duk Kim, Benjamin Bryant,
Paolo Montalban

Donna Murphy

Joohee Choi, Lou Diamond Phillips

Act 1 Finale: Donna Murphy, Lou Diamond Phillips, Company

The March of the Siamese Children:
**Kelly Jordan Bit, Lou Diamond Phillips,
Donna Murphy**

The Royal Children

Royal Children and Wives

Getting To Know You:
Donna Murphy, Royal
Children and Wives

We Kiss in a Shadow:
Joohee Choi, Jose Llana

1996 Outer Critics Circle Award:
Outstanding Debut of an Actor –
Lou Diamond Phillips

1996 Tony® Award:
Best Performance by a Leading Actress
in a Musical – Donna Murphy

Something Wonderful: Taewon Kim

The Small House of Uncle Thomas:
Tito Abeleda and Ensemble

I Have Dreamed: Jose Llana, Joohee Choi

Procession of the White Elephant

Shall We Dance? Lou Diamond Phillips and Donna Murphy

MY LORD AND MASTER

Lyrics by OSCAR HAMMERSTEIN II
Music by RICHARD RODGERS

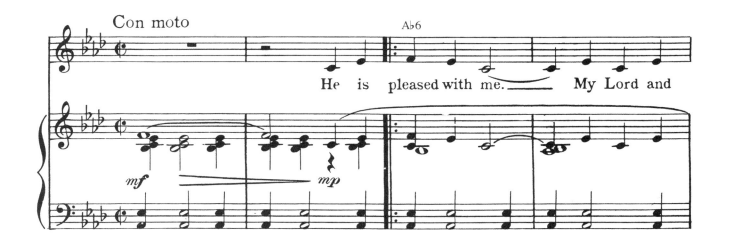

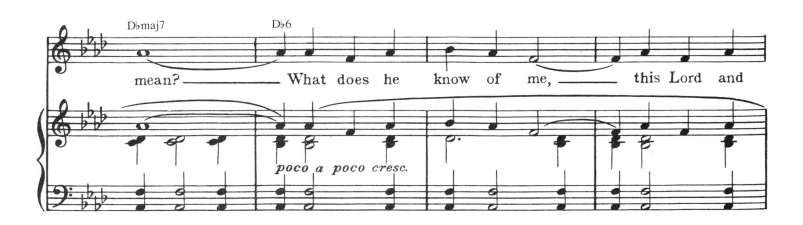

HELLO, YOUNG LOVERS

Lyrics by OSCAR HAMMERSTEIN II
Music by RICHARD RODGERS

THE MARCH OF THE SIAMESE CHILDREN

Lyrics by OSCAR HAMMERSTEIN II
Music by RICHARD RODGERS

GETTING TO KNOW YOU

Lyrics by OSCAR HAMMERSTEIN II
Music by RICHARD RODGERS

It's a ver-y an-cient say-ing But a true and hon-est thought, That if you be-come a teach-er, by your pu-pils you'll be taught. As a teach-er, I've been

WE KISS IN A SHADOW

Lyrics by OSCAR HAMMERSTEIN II
Music by RICHARD RODGERS

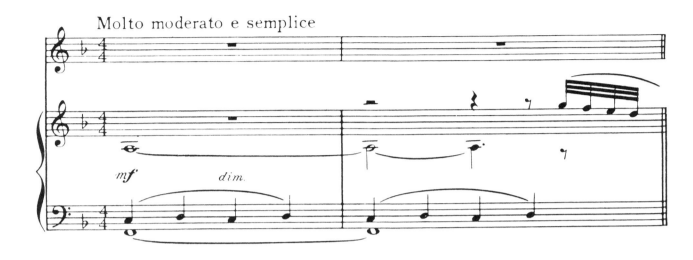

SOMETHING WONDERFUL

Lyrics by OSCAR HAMMERSTEIN II
Music by RICHARD RODGERS

I HAVE DREAMED

Lyrics by OSCAR HAMMERSTEIN II
Music by RICHARD RODGERS

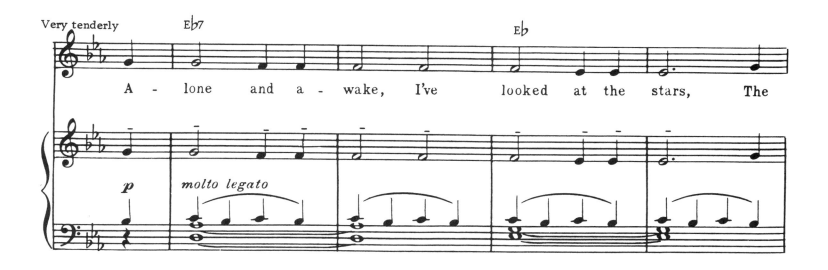

A - lone and a - wake, I've looked at the stars, The

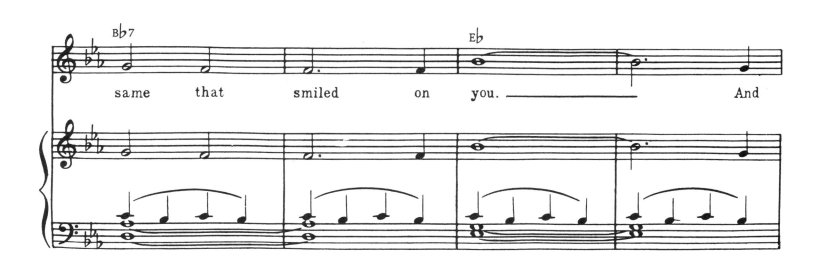

same that smiled on you. _____ And

SHALL WE DANCE?

Lyrics by OSCAR HAMMERSTEIN II
Music by RICHARD RODGERS

We've just been in-tro-duced, I do not know you well. But when the mu-sic start-ed, some-thing drew me to your side. So

NEIL SIMON THEATRE

Dodger Productions
The John F. Kennedy Center for the Performing Arts
James M. Nederlander, Perseus Productions with John Frost and the Adelaide Festival Centre
in association with The Rodgers and Hammerstein Organization
present

Donna Murphy   Lou Diamond Phillips

in

Rodgers and Hammerstein's

THE KING
and
I.

Music by
Richard Rodgers

Book and Lyrics by
Oscar Hammerstein II

Based upon the novel *Anna and the King of Siam* by
Margaret Landon

with

Randall Duk Kim   Taewon Kim   Joohee Choi   Jose Llana
John Curless   Guy Paul   Ryan Hopkins   John Chang

Tito Abeleda   John Bantay   Camille M. Brown   Benjamin Bryant   Meng-Chen Chang
Kam Cheng   Vivien Eng   Lydia Gaston   Margaret Ann Gates   Devanand N. Janki
Susan Kikuchi   C. Sean Kim   Shawn Ku   Doan Mackenzie   Barbara McCulloh
Paolo Montalban   Alan Muraoka   Paul Nakauchi   Tina Ou   Andrew Pacho
Mami Saito   Lainie Sakakura   Tran T. Thuc Hanh   Carol To   Yolanda Tolentino
Joan Tsao   Yan Ying   Kayoko Yoshioka   Greg Zane

Kelly Jordan Bit   Lexine Bondoc   Kailip Boonrai   Jonathan Giordano
Jacqueline Te Lem   Erik Lin-Greenberg   Kenji Miyata   Brandon Marshall Ngai
Amy Y. Tai   Jenna Noelle Ushkowitz   Shelby Rebecca Wong   Jeff G. Yalun

Scenic Design	Costume Design	Lighting Design
Brian Thomson	**Roger Kirk**	**Nigel Levings**

Sound by
Tony Meola and **Lewis Mead**

Hair by
David H. Lawrence

Orchestrations	Musical Supervision	Music Direction
Robert Russell Bennett	**Eric Stern**	**Michael Rafter**

Additional Orchestrations	Music Coordinator	Casting
Bruce Coughlin	**John Miller**	**Jay Binder**

Production Stage Manager	Production Supervision	Marketing Consultant	Press Representative
Frank Hartenstein	**Gene O'Donovan**	**Margery Singer**	**Boneau/Bryan-Brown**

Executive Producer	Associate Producers	Associate General Manager
Dodger Productions	**Abbey Butler** and **Melvyn J. Estrin**	**Robert C. Strickstein**
	Hal Luftig	

Musical Staging by
Lar Lubovitch

Choreography by
Jerome Robbins

Directed by
Christopher Renshaw

I WHISTLE A HAPPY TUNE

Lyrics by OSCAR HAMMERSTEIN II
Music by RICHARD RODGERS